Benedict Canfield

The holy will of God

A short rule of perfection

Benedict Canfield

The holy will of God
A short rule of perfection

ISBN/EAN: 9783741164255

Manufactured in Europe, USA, Canada, Australia, Japa

Cover: Foto ©Lupo / pixelio.de

Manufactured and distributed by brebook publishing software
(www.brebook.com)

Benedict Canfield

The holy will of God

THE

HOLY WILL OF GOD:

A

Short Rule of Perfection.

BY THE

REV. FATHER BENEDICT CANFIELD,

CAPUCHIN FRIAR.

TRANSLATED BY

FATHER COLLINS.

"In His Will is Life." —Ps. xxix.____

LONDON:
THOMAS RICHARDSON AND SONS.
26, PATERNOSTER ROW; AND DERBY.
1878.

The Holy Ghost is the Uncreated Will of God. His devout servants cannot honour Him better than by making their wills uniform with this Divine Will. This Will of God was our Lord's normal rule of conduct when on earth. He says: "I do always those things that please Him;" and again: "Not My Will but Thine be done." By willing what God wills we come to have "the mind of Christ," and being joined to the Lord, have one Spirit with Him.

THE TRANSLATOR.

The Rule of Perfection.

—✠—

PART I.

Containing the Rule of Perfection, and the mode of knowing and Exercising its degrees.

CHAPTER I.

Proposing and Explaining of this Rule.

SECTION I.

THE sum of the practice of the whole of this rule is, that we should do our works, and every action, for the sake of God's only Will, and to please Him. I say, all our works and actions, that I may comprehend all, both bodily and spiritual, our thoughts, words, and works; whether by driving away temptations, or by following inspirations; whether by casting away vices and imperfections, or by being industrious in virtue; by speaking or silence, toiling or resting, struggling with ill-success or enjoying prosperity, bearing afflictions or tasting consolations. Nay, further, I include things natural as well as things supernatural, little as well as great, mean and vile with what is lofty and excellent. In short, I embrace everything that is done by every power, whether of soul or body; everything that is endured on any side soever. All these things are to be done, or to be endured, for the only end of fulfilling the Divine Will, and with this only intention, "Because God so wills." No exception is to be made at all, whether of thing, time, place, or person.

The forenamed intention comprises six degrees and perfections, viz.: that it be made actually, singly, gladly, unhesitatingly, clearly, and promptly.

SECTION II.

By the first degree, termed *actually*, is denoted the *actual* remembrance of the Divine Will, as set in the elevation of the mind to God, and in the direction of the intention according to the same Divine Will.

By this degree forgetfulness is shut out in the undertaking of any work, spiritual or bodily, since this forgetfulness is a common mistake, which causes immense loss, robbing us of an incredible treasure of light and. grace, and of an unknown weight of merit and glory.

However, when we would avoid the extreme of forgetfulness, we must beware of running into the opposite excess of too much remembrance, by making manifold acts, and by so frequently exactly recalling the intention as to bewilder the brain. When, therefore, I say that each single work is to be directed by the intention, I do not mean every trivial action that is accomplished by any member of the body, the senses, or the mental faculties; I only mean such works as are distinguished and separated from one another: and these only when a person begins them, and when he discovers that he is drawn away from God, and is no longer mindful of the Divine Will: but not so long as his mind is raised up on high.

But especial care is to be taken not to give over to forgetfulness such things as we know to be very pleasing to nature,

or very unpleasing; for here turns the
hinge. The sum of spiritual profit consists in this care. Still, again, a person
should not be scrupulous, if he perceive
that in this, as in other degrees, he is
defective. He should not accuse himself
as if he had fallen into some sin therefore ; for the desire of reducing this rule
into practice makes it in no way more
binding upon him than it was before.

SECTION III.

The second degree of this pure intention is *singly:* that is, that this Will
should be put before us as the only simple and single end, which induces us
either to the doing or suffering of a
thing. This degree shuts out all other
ends, of what kind soever ; not bad and
froward ends only, such as pride, envy,
&c. ; or such ends as are stained by
some imperfection, as the doing a thing
for the respect and favour of men, self-
love, self-pleasing, sensuality ; in short,
all venial sins, and whatsoever has the
blot of imperfection : but it shuts out
even those intentions which in themselves would be good, but which, along-

side of what is of more perfection, lose
their price, and are found imperfect.
Under this class might be ranked bodily
penances, disciplines, fastings, either to
escape hell, or to deserve reward or paradise, &c. This degree, therefore, has a
peculiar relation to the deadening of all
the passions, our affections, self-love, and
all other imperfections whatsoever. To
this work every devout soul ought to
apply her whole strength. For all spiritual progress turns upon this. Through
this a solid foundation has to be laid in
the beginning, a safe progress to be
sought in the journey, and a finished perfection in the end of the entire active life.

SECTION IV.

The third degree is *gladly;* to wit,
that not only should a work be done
singly for the Will of God, but gladly too,
and with a full assent, joined with a certain peace and tranquillity, and so with
a spiritual gladness arising therefrom :
that by reason of this the soul may be
rendered capable of the presence of God,
and of the influence of the Holy Spirit.
For David says : "His place is in peace ;"

that is, in a soul hushed from any din of
the affections, untroubled by the tumult
of the passions, unshaken by the motions
of unbridled desires. By this degree "gladly," all sadness
is shut out, sorrow or contradiction,
whether in doing of any thing, or leaving
it undone, or in enduring something, &c.,
from whatsoever source such a contradiction flows; whether from the low, mean
nature in the thing commanded, as e.g.
taking care of sick people, or performing
household duties, &c., or from its being
tiresome and difficult, or dishonourable,
in a worldly point of view, &c. Or again,
from the work itself being of a laborious
kind, and incapable of being done without perplexity. The work may be disagreeable on account of the time when
it is ordered to be done, as for instance,
if we be told to work when we wish to
rest, or be told to rest when we would
wish to work, &c. The work may be disagreeable because of the publicity of the
place where it is done, or the unpleasant-
ness of the place, &c. Or we may dislike
it under pretext of piety, of prayer, fasting, discipline, study, preaching, &c. For
some, if the Superior gives an order which

breaks into their private exercises, obey
with an ill grace, unwillingly and reluc-
tantly; their own will persuading them
that the exercise in which they were em-
ployed was much better. And so blind
do they thus become as to be unable to
see how much " better is obedience than
sacrifice." They do not perceive that
these works, though excellent in themselves, are of no value at all when done
contrary to the Will of God, which is
made known to them by His law, and by
the commandment, or known intention,
of the Superior, when he orders anything
not contrary to God's law.

There is another species of contradiction which has its source in causes far
more hidden than all. In this case,
when a person knows a work to be the
Will of God he girds himself *gladly* to
the task, yet spends his mind, time, and
labour unwillingly, to execute it with
faithfulness. So he turns aside his mind
rather towards God and His Will; in
doing which he neglects the work, and
does not bring it to its finish with due
perfection. This is a mistake which de-
serves well marking, and is of a very
secret sort. For the mind, indeed, being

drawn off from the work, that it may pass like a dart into the Will of God, a distinction is thus made between the work and God's Will, as if the work were one thing, and God's Will another, when in fact they are but one and the same thing; so that it falls out that God, being sought outside of the work, is sought outside of His own Will.

Now, when God is so sought, the more He is sought the less He is found, since He is never found by working in a way opposed to His Will. He is found only by His Will, that is, by doing what He orders: *in* His Will, that is, His own work: by the help of His Will, that is, by performing it, and that *gladly*, with the whole mind, and the whole strength, according to our bounden duty, by which we are tied to serve Him with all our heart and strength, not sadly or of necessity, for God loveth a cheerful giver.

Let it then be laid down as a most solid foundation of all this business, so often as anything occurs to be done, whether ghostly or bodily, that that very work, so far as respects him who has to do it, is itself the Will of God, and is to him " spirit and life." I say " that very work" to designate the thing to be done, and to shut out all images whatsoever of other things. I add, "whether ghostly or bodily," lest any one should falsely imagine that one rather than the other is rejected. I do so also, that thus quietly, by the way, a complete extinguisher may be put on the abuse of many, who set about a spiritual work more gladly than about a bodily one, fancying one to be more excellent than the other, and thinking to draw more light from the one than from the other. Now, viewed in themselves this may be perfectly true; nor is it an ill thing to prefer one work to another, when we have free power of choosing either. But when the Will of God comes in, by reason of some command or obligation, then it is otherwise; then it is an abuse to prefer spiritual things to corporal, since, as was said above, "obedience is better than sacrifice."

I add further, in respect of him who has to work, that the substance of the work, whether it be bodily or ghostly, is, together with its accidents, &c., to be shut out from consideration, since these are not the Will of God. But the work

ought to be known by his mind simply as
God's Will and good pleasure without
division. This is done by his making up
two things into a single one : that is, its
being known on the one hand that the
doing of the work is God's true Will ; and
on the other, that God's Will is the exe-
cution of the work. Thus the work itself
is the very Will of God ; and, in such
sort, is, to him that works, spirit and life.

SECTION V.

The fourth degree attributed to this
perfect intention is called *unhesitatingly.*
This gives to the intention a certain sureness, by which it is fortified and made
strong. It consists in this, that when
the person has directed the work he has
in hand to the sole aim of God's Will, he
with an unhesitating faith holds it to be
God's Will. This degree of sureness
shuts out all wavering, and every sort of
doubt.

Of doubts there are for the most part
three causes. The first cause is in indifferent things, when a person knows not
which side to choose, as the more pleasing to God, in the doing of a thing or

leaving it undone. The second is, when it is a small matter, or even so vile and mean that many are persuaded that it has no place with God at all. They would, in a manner, say: "*Surely, God is very anxious whether it be this or that;*" or, "*What has God to do with such like trifles?*" The third is in matters which regard the senses and pleasure, as eating, drinking, and the like. For some, I am aware, fancy they would act insincerely and hypocritically, or even in a sort be making a mockery with God, were they to say that they did only for His Will and good pleasure things which are agreeable and grateful to the senses.

Now, in order to meet these cases, we must know that, for the first, a judgment concerning indifferent matters is to be formed, not through the outward matter in itself, but by a discussion within the mind; that is, by contemplating and examining the intention. If the intention is right, and aims at the Will of God, then that thing is really taken which is conformable to the same Will. For in matters indifferent the intention gives its character to the work, not the work to the intention. More will be said of this further on. As regards other matters the apostolic warning must be borne in mind : " *All things whatsoever ye do, in word or work, do all in the Name of the Lord Jesus Christ.*" When he says *all* he leaves out nothing, however small. Saint Augustine also, on Psalm cxlvi., for the same purpose says : " Thou praisest God by doing thy business ; thou praisest Him by taking meat and drink ; thou praisest Him by resting in bed ; thou praisest Him by sleeping."

SECTION VI.

The fifth degree of this intention we laid down as *clearly ;* by which is meant that a lively faith goes with it : and just as we know the work so done to be the Will of God, so with a lively faith, a *clear* eye, and steadfast gaze, we contemplate it as such. The mind ought to see the work, not as "*this work,*" but as "*this Will ;*" not as an outward work, but as the inward good pleasure of God. It should look at it, not as something created, but as the Uncreated Will of God. For, just as God wishes the work to be done, so He asks that it be done, not as a

work, but as His Will. The mind, then,
ought, in the work, to regard God's Will
alone.

By this degree all that sleepy dulness
of faith is cast away, which many times
puts great obstacles in the way of our
spiritual advancement, sadly robbing our
souls of the light and knowledge of God;
so that our wills are not kindled with
this burning love, nor our minds en-
snared by this beauty, ennobled by the
lofty majesty, or, in fine, stirred up by
the quickening Spirit of God; but we
slumber away, living in the darksomeness
and destitution of mere nature : and all
because we neglect to put in practice what
we know, and to stretch out our faith to
that which we believe.

By this degree, however, of lively
faith, and by the actual view, fixed contemplation, and sight of the Divine Will,
all this wretchedness departs. The sha-
dows flee away, the darksomeness wholly
vanishes, and the soul remains vividly
attentive to this Will, united to God in a
manner inexpressible, enlightened, quick-
ened, and elevated.

SECTION VII.

The sixth degree of this perfection is termed *promptly.* By which is meant that the direction of the intention, enriched by the foregoing degrees, becomes nimble and unembarrassed, so that it is not delayed till the end, or even the middle of the work, but is made at its very outset and entrance gate.

This degree shakes off all tardiness, and allows of no delays whatsoever in the making of our intention right, when we set about the doing or finishing any work. Such delays not unfrequently steal from us all the profit and desert of our work, whilst we are, on occasions, leaning in our work to some less worthy intention than is the only Will of God. Sometimes we are altogether destitute of any right intention. We even become guilty of a fault, and sin by having a bad intention for what we do or suffer. The source of all these evils is the want of quickness and diligence in at once examining our intention at the very outset. Any defect that may have occurred, by

reason of such-like torpor, should be re-
paired, as far as our power goes, by
amending our intention, so soon as we
discover that it has gone astray from the
right path.

SECTION VIII.

It is to be noted, further, that we may
fail of the later degrees of this intention,
though those that go before are perfect.
We cannot, however, fail in one or more
of the first degrees without spoiling all
the rest that follow, because, where the
less perfection is wanting, the greater is
never present. To fail in the first degrees brings, therefore, greater damage
than a failure in the later ones.

If, however, any one perceives at the
beginning of a work, that he has fallen
into some of these defects, he should not
cast away all hope of perseverance, but
remembering the proverb, *Better late than
never*, he should, as the work advances,
or before its finish, change this crooked
intention into a right one, forming it
according to the degrees laid down, and
correcting by the normal rule of the
Divine Will, every defect, through the
degree opposed to it.

It is only right that to this point the whole mind, all care, diligence, and watchfulness should be applied whilst working. The intention should be examined and laid bare with the scruti- nizing glance of the soul, to search if all these degrees are there, to see whether the intention, through lack of some of the degrees, has its beauty sullied by some defiling blot of self-love, or the lustre of its splendour bedimmed by some darkening cloud of self-will.

The only excellence and advantage to be found in this direction and examina- tion of the intention, is in its being the shortest cut, and most direct route, to the climax of perfection. For it leads us by the hand, as it were, to self-knowledge, uncovering the hidden fund of self-love, laying bare unsuspected passions, bring- ing out lurking affections from their secret covert, and pointing out our im- perfections as it were with the finger. Through lack of this exact examination, serious care, and never-ceasing search into the inner chambers of the soul, there are many who lodge passions there, thinking them to be inspirations; they admit many affections fancying they are

holy impulses; their self-love they imagine to be love of God; and when they
follow the will of the old Adam, they are
induced to believe they are led by the
desire of the new.

In this examination let not any one
give an over-easy belief; nor because, at
his first glance within, he has discovered
nothing which seems to require the file,
let him on that account suppose that all
is surely well with him; for such a
thing happens often from lack of light,
not freedom from faultiness. There is
plenty of self-love, but the sharp eye to
see it is wanting. This light and this
sharpness of vision those will surely reach
who abide continually within their souls.
For just as when one comes into a dark-
some chamber from the noonday blaze of
the sun, at his first entrance he can see
nothing; but if he tarry but a little
while he thoroughly sees all that lay hid :
so is it with the soul. When from the
tumult and din of outer affairs she be-
takes herself into the inner room of the
heart she beholds nothing. But waiting
a little while within, she presently sees
all that is imperfect. Here then you
have the six degrees of a perfect intention.

CHAPTER II.

**Of the mode whereby this Will of God is
known and brought into practice.**

SECTION I.

ALL things that have to be done or
suffered, admitted or rejected, whether
they be bodily or ghostly, are of three
kinds, viz. things *commanded,* things *forbidden,* or things *indifferent.* Nothing
can chance which is not contained under
one of these headings.

As regards the first, if what is *commanded* is such as we have debated about,
the Will of God is most clearly evident,
to wit, that it should be done. We ought
therefore to perform it, and that according to the foresaid general rule, namely,
because God so wills, putting aside every
other end.

For the second, if a thing be *forbidden,*
the Will of God is no less plain : to wit,
that it must not be done. It is therefore
to be left undone, simply because such is
the Divine Will. Other motives, of what
sort soever, are to be rejected, and so far
as can be, blotted clean out of the mind.

As regards the third sort, *things indifferent*, they may be divided into three kinds. Some are agreeable to nature or to the senses, such as to talk of curious things, to hear news, to see beautiful sights, and the like. Nature dislikes other things, such as silence, keeping fasts that are not commanded, etc. Other things, again, nature is indifferent about; as, for instance, to go in by this road or that, to sit or to walk, and all things the contrary of which would be equally agreeable.

Now, of the first sort of things, when those who would fulfil God's Will meet with anything pleasant to the senses and likeable, they should reject it. If it belongs to the second sort, and is disagreeable to the senses, they should embrace it. These maxims are borne out by Holy Writ, which in almost every page exhorts us to put to death the old Adam. So Coloss. iii. : " *Mortify your members that are upon the earth.*" Rom. viii. : " *But if by the Spirit ye mortify the deeds of the flesh, ye shall live.*"

This caution must meanwhile however be given, that watch be kept, whether discretion, true or feigned, does not re-

quire the contrary, either for health's
sake, or because of the person, the time,
place, and other like things. Now, if
such circumstances exist, and doubtful
reasons on both sides, so that it is not
known which side to take, to do or to
leave undone, to resist or to consent,
then it is best to take up with one side or
other without more ado, always however
keeping to the forenamed intention of
the Will of God. This is to be done,
because it is not possible to make lengthy
deliberation without much distraction,
confusion of the brain, and loss of time,
unless, which rarely happens, the case be
of such importance as to deserve it. In
this case recourse is to be had, both to
the prayers of devout souls and to the
counsel of learned and judicious men.

If the thing belong to the third class,
that is, be simply indifferent, and to do
it or leave it be neither agreeable nor disagreeable to the senses, then it will be
lawful to turn either this way or that,
always however presupposing the Will of
God. We may then use these or other
like words: *I will do or leave this undone ; I will accept or refuse this, because
it is Thy Will.* When this has been·

done, then what was indifferent becomes the Will of God, just as much as the doing or not doing things because commanded or forbidden. The reason is, because the intention gives its character to the work, so that things, neither commanded nor forbidden, receive their goodness or badness from the quality of the intention.

SECTION II.

But in order to bring into practice this rule, we must not suppose that the chief business lies in searching out what is the Will of God in all things. The profit does not consist in knowing it, but in doing it; not in nicely discussing it in every doubtful matter, but in the faithful performance of it in cases plain and evident. Of this sort are such things as hang on our own judgment and will, which are every moment occurring; things that we do or leave undone simply through some passion or affection, contrary to the Will of God plainly evidenced to the soul. In these things we must strive, with might and main, to show ourselves faithful to the practice of this rule.

In this point lies the whole gist of our spiritual advancement.

It must further be noted that, when we speak of things commanded or forbidden, we do not mean any weighty matters, the doing or leaving undone of which would be a mortal sin. We intend only such lighter things, the doing or neglecting of which would be a venial fault or imperfection. For our speech is here not only of the keeping of God's commandments, but of the path of perfection, which chiefly consists in the eschewing of imperfections. For he would grievously err, whoever, under pretext of spirituality or contemplation, should neglect any of the forementioned things, commanded or forbidden by the decrees, constitutions, orders, intentions, and laws of Superiors, however trivial the matter might be. For how can it be that that should tend to perfection, which turns from obedience, and nurses self-love, the root of all imperfection? Or how will that ever make increase of perfection, which lessens the fulfilment of one's profession. As, however, it happens that things are commanded which seem agreeable to nature and the senses, such as eating, drinking,

play and recreation, &c., and things unpleasant to the senses and to our taste
are forbidden, such as fasting, labour,
and other toilsome, hard, rude, and disagreeable things; it is of all importance
in such like cases that the intention be
firmly kept from the defiling stain of
sensuality, or from being wounded and
weakened by the violence and impetuosity
of uncurbed affections. This may be
brought about by making contrary acts,
that is, by renouncing the pleasure felt,
and by drawing the mind off another
way; by closing all the entrances of the
spiritual powers against the like pleasure,
and by darting in opposition all their
force into God. Thus the soul offers
herself to God as a vessel by which He
may accomplish the work she does for
His own honour only, and for His will,
without respect to any advantage the
creature may get thereby. It comes to
pass, by this means, that the soul, which
would otherwise be seeking her delights
rather from the sensual and pleasing
nature of the thing done than from God's
Will, does now, on the contrary, after a
spiritual act made in this wise, place all
her delight in the only Will of God.

2

But if, after all, in these things which
are commanded, or in other things done
with true discretion, the soul feels still
some delight or pleasure, little or much,
contrary to reason and the purity of this
intention, and the rebellious movement
remains, even when she resists it by
making acts the opposite way, let her not
lose heart, or be be discouraged, or fancy,
as many do, that all is lost, or that she
cannot have resisted firmly enough ; she
ought rather to remain stout-hearted,
being most surely persuaded that she has
never been overcome, unless she so willed
it herself, by the consent of the higher
and more spiritual part of the soul.

Such conflicts as these within her let
the soul take as from God's hand, that
is, as being His Will, and the cross of
Christ. For she must not veil from sight
that the cross is to be found, not only in
injuries sustained from without, but in
combats also within. He well knew this
who said (Job vii.) : "*I am become bur-
densome to myself;*" as also he who says
(Rom. vii.) : "*I see another law in my
members, warring against the law of my
mind, and captivating me in the law of
sin.*"

CHAPTER III.

Of the peculiar mode of entering into the practice of this exercise, of persisting in it with fruit, and of making advance in it.

SECTION I.

LET him who means to give himself to the practice of this exercise lay upon himself a certain task, not binding himself to it under pain of sin, either mortal or venial, but only tied by the bond of a firm resolve. Let this task be a certain number of mortifications and self-denials, to be completed each day, to comply with God's good pleasure; three, five, or ten, according to his fervour and devotion. These are to be made up by denying something to one or other of the senses or faculties of the body or the soul. The body may be mortified in the five senses, sight, hearing, smell, taste, and touch; by doing or suffering what is unpleasant and disagreeable to them: for instance, when a person wishes to look at some beautiful thing, to take a

view of some nice place, pleasant gardens,
superb towers, and such-like pleasant
spectacles: or again, when a person
would be glancing his eyes here and
there through curiosity, which curiosity
distracts him from God. In all these
things the sight is to be mortified, our
own will being renounced for the sake of
the Will of God.

In like manner, the desire of hearing
harmonious tunes is to be mortified, or
the hearing of some new curious instrument, or anything that may delight the
ears. So also is the appetite to be mortified, when any one is led to take food or
drinks that are dainty, delicious fruits, or
any other thing that flatters the taste,
even though it should not be either rare
or costly.

To the smell, in like manner, are all
perfumes to be refused, and all other
things not so evidently agreeable.

From the touch all soft things, and
such as might raise sensual motions, are
to be retrenched. From all the senses
occasion may be taken every day of renouncing self for the Will of God, by
rejecting everything pleasurable, and offering it according to the rules laid down as

a glad sacrifice to God; saying with the prophet, " *Willingly will I sacrifice.*" On the contrary, those things which are hateful to the senses are to be accepted, viz. what is unpleasant to the sight, disagreeable to the hearing, loathsome to the smell, bitter to the taste, uneasy and rough to the touch.

The faculties of the soul do also give us means for mortification. We may, to comply with God's Will, renounce worldly discourse and intellectual speculations, refusing to the understanding the vain pleasure it might find in them. We may cast out of our memory the thought of the sins and imperfections of our neighbour, and the wrongs done by him to us, as also the remembrance of indecent or unseemly words, actions, and gestures.

In the same manner we may mortify the will in all its unbridled passions, and in its affections that pass due measure. These, according to philosophy, are of two classes. In respect of good, there are love, desire, joy: in respect of ill, hate, flight, and sadness. These six passions are seated in the concupiscence. Hope, despair, fear, boldness, and anger are lodged in the irascible part. They may

be all classed under four heads : vain joy,
vain hope, vain sadness, vain fear, as
summed up in these verses :

"If with clear eye thou wouldst see truth alone,
Bid fear, joy, hope, and sadness to begone."

To this mortification of the will belongs
also the resistance that must be made to
all temptations to sin : as, for instance,
to pride, in which soil are rooted all the
other trees. Then vain glory comes with
its branches, ostentation, hypocrisy, strife,
obstinacy, discord, invention of novelties.
Envy, with its offspring, hate, whisper-
ing, detraction, joy at our neighbour's ill
fortune, and sadness at his success.
Anger, with its children, indignation,
swelling of heart, clamour, blasphemy,
abuse, strife. Sloth, with its progeny,
malice, rancour, cowardice, despair, care-
lessness, and distraction. Avarice, with
her brood, treachery, cheating, falsehood,
violence, perjury, restlessness, and hard-
ness of heart. Gluttony, with her fol-
lowers, silly joy, buffoonery, uncleanness,
talkativeness and stupidity. Lust, last of
all, with her company, blindness of
heart, thoughtlessness, rashness, incon-
tinence, love of self, hatred of God, affection for this world, and horror of the next.

All these sins, and the temptations to
them, supply matter for self-denial. On
all sides, therefore, whether it be in
matters of the body or of the soul, there
are plenty of opportunities for the exercise of this practice, so very evident that
the veriest tyro ,and novice cannot but put
his finger upon them.

Beginners, therefore, for their instruction, and in order to get themselves into
the practice as well as others, to press on
and keep it up, should set themselves a
certain number of mortifications daily,
from the above cited things. They should
pick out especially the points in which
they know themselves to be weak, renouncing in them their own will for the
sake of the Will of God. They should
remember to examine well whether in
each their pure intention was built and
stablished on the aforesaid six degrees.
By this means beginners will get a true
knowledge of their inward souls, a thing
of the utmost importance and absolutely
necessary. The others also will gain
much fruit by keeping up their practice ;
so that both one and the other will make
an immense advancement.

SECTION II.

There are two especial modes of con-
tinuing the purity of this intention. The
first is suited to beginners, the other to
those who have made some progress.
But if what beginners are wanting in they
make up for by serious care and diligence,
then both these modes may equally be
found to suit each class.

The first mode consists in making
various acts within the soul. Of these,
in the first place comes the act of filial
fear; an act of deep reverence towards
God, the soul seeing Him to be so near ·
to her, and that she is by His power so
illumined, so wrapped up in His bright-
ness, and as it were on all sides girt by
the dazzling ray of His Godhead and its
lustrous splendours.

At other times she may make an act of
deep humility and submission of herself,
beholding the succour given to her own
wretchedness by the evident protection of
God, and seeing her unworthiness so
waited on by the very Presence of God,
that not without reason she cries out with

Peter: "*Depart from me, for I am a siuful man, O Lord.*"

Then, again, she may give way to a sovereign admiration, joy and gladness of heart, in seeing that she is made a living instrument and temple of God.

She may also, by a certain sweet inclination full of love, bow herself to her heavenly Bridegroom, as she earnestly desires His marvellous clemency and goodness.

She may also be filled with immense gladness of soul to behold how she has been set free from the slavery of self, and has got out of the prison of her own will.

She may also, by an utter and absolute abandonment, resign herself into the hands of her Bridegroom, thus more fully and completely to enjoy Him.

She may make acts of an eternal renouncement of self, as having learned by experience how inebriating are the consolations, and how rich the fruits, that most certainly flow therefrom.

Sometimes she may annihilate herself at the view of the Almighty and Endless Being of God, so far away from her, yet so near.

She may pour herself forth in endless

sacred sighs, willing to have her conver-
sation always in heaven, whilst she beholds those bonds of her own will which
once kept her glued to the earth, now
broken in sunder.

She may closely knit herself to God by
love, feeling the flames of His charity
intimately and sweetly consuming her.

To conclude, she may occupy herself
intently with the thought of that union
between God and the soul, which is
brought about by the two wills being at
unity in work. She may keep up, nurse,
and cherish this union by ever listening
to, gladly following, and readily obeying
the drawing of the same Spirit of God.

The other mode of keeping the intention in its entirety pure and perfect—and
this mode touches more nearly its essence—is a sort of surrender of all owner-
ship in the work. To do this, when the
intention has been rightly carried through
all its degrees, whether the work be an
outward one or within the soul, then she
ought to strip herself of it, as indeed in
no way hers. This stripping consists,
after completing the direction of the intention, in plainly bringing the mind to
work not its own will, but the Divine

Will, to follow not its own spirit but the
Spirit of God. The work then conse-
quently is fulfilled, not by itself but by
God, the soul being but an instrument of
His, though a willing one ; but even this
she has not from herself but from God.

A work thus accomplished she ought
therefore to look upon fixedly as His very
Will and working, and as the Spirit of
of God, as laid down in the fourth
degree. Not only indeed ought the soul
to contemplate the work as the real Will
of God, but she should cleave to it as
such, and abide in it, all contention being
gathered up. Thus made firm and settled immoveably in it, all worldly din and
the tumult of the passions being driven
far away into exile, in sovereign peace
and calm deep silence the soul attends to
the Light of Heaven, and in vast abund-
ance drinks in this Spirit of the Divine
Will. For to her this Spirit is her future
light and life, her peace and joy, abode
and rest, her rule and perfection, her
wealth and treasure, her beginning and
last end. The six degrees of this perfect
intention she will thus in continuance
fill up, and by a settled perseverance she
will stablish in herself that throne, on

which she may invite the Sovereign
King Solomon, her heavenly Bridegroom,
sweetly to take His rest.

SECTION III.

To crown this first part we will set
forth an instruction as to the mode of
prayer suitable to this exercise.

There are four modes of prayer, from
which should be taken by each one that
particular kind best fitted to his own disposition and capabilities. Of these the
first is vocal prayer, the most imperfect
kind of all, as having the smallest measure of light. This prayer suits novices
and beginners.

The second, mental prayer, especially
on the most sacred Passion of Christ, is
better than the former, as having more
light. This serves for those who have
made some progress.

The third is the prayer of aspirations,
that is, of short fervent little prayers,
and ardent sighs or desires, sometimes
breaking forth from the heart only, sometimes also from the mouth. This prayer
is very much more perfect than those
before mentioned, as made with less

labour of the understanding. This kind those are wont to use who have made no little progress.

The fourth sort of prayer is that which consists in a settled cleaving to the Will of God alone, without meditation or vocal prayer. This kind is far the best of all, for those who are capable of it, as being founded and stablished on the pure love of God and charity. This kind fits those whose minds are all on fire, made simple, and stripped bare of all images and sensible things. It may suit also those who, though not yet arrived at this height of perfection, do, by strenuous mind, and patient waiting for the touch of the Holy Spirit, supply what is lacking to them by occasional aspirations; these aspirations being, however, of a very subtle, deep, and spiritual nature.

And let not such be discouraged in mind, believing themselves to waste their time idly, when they so persist in the presence of God, prostrate at the Feet of the Crucified: for the soul is by this means far more profited; her acts are deeper and more spiritual; her self-oblation is greater; and more sweetly is the holocaust of the whole man offered. In

3

short, she pleases God better than when sailing on wings through the midst of heaven she makes the most lovely discourses on divine and profound mysteries. The soul which God vouchsafes to visit, after duly waiting and disposing herself in this sort, will find herself at one single time more filled with light than by a hundred others, when she did not work after this fashion.

As regards those who have not yet got so far as to be fit for this fourth sort of prayer, but who labour to practice, according to their capacity, one of the other kinds, these ought still, in the use of it, to observe the tenor of this rule. By this is meant that they should, in all their vocal prayers, meditations, and aspirations, set before themselves, entirely and singly, as their aim, the Divine Will alone. This Divine Will should be the only desire of their heart; and no comfort or light ought they to seek in their prayer, except so far as it shall please God. He who shall so do will get immense joy. For he will find the single object of his vows, namely, the Will of God. In this business it is wont to happen that he who sought his own comfort most secures the least; and on the contrary, he who lets go all comfort for the sake of God's only Will, receives comfort in most full and ample measure.

For those who would fashion their meditations, aspirations and contemplations to the square of this rule, six points or inward acts are necessary.

1. To protest that we come to prayer for God's Will alone, and to please Him, with no seeking after comfort, light, etc. But fearful and scrupulous souls ought not to fancy this protestation to bind them under pain of sin, mortal or venial, it being only in quality of a good purpose, not a promise that binds.

2. To turn inward the gaze of the soul, examining with strict search to the very core of the heart, and judging with all fairness whether the protestation is a true one or not. This examination should be most exact, and the judgment formed impartial. He that is faithful in this point, and can pierce the deep abyss of the heart, will have opened for himself the gate to perfect contemplation.

3. To prune and strip off anything that may be discovered contrary to this protestation ; doing violence to self-love, which

perpetually provokes and solicits the soul
to long for sensible comfort, or at least
for that which is spiritual.

4. Clinging ever to this Will of God as
the base and end of her prayer, the soul
is not to care so much for making beautiful discourses, or for gaining fervour and
devotion, or even for rendering her prayer
perfect to her own point of view, as to
bend herself to this Divine Will, and
abandon herself to it in entire union with
it, nestling it in her mind, lavishing on it
all her love, and worshipping it with a
deep veneration.

5. From time to time, with a simple
short glance, to visit this protestation and
examine it, to see if perhaps it comes
short of its first purity, and particularly if
any loathing or weariness has arisen in
the soul.

6. To think enough has been done, and
to conceive on this account a certain deep
and serene gladness of mind at the ending
of the prayer, whether it were dry or
devout, because the soul has obtained
what she longed after, namely, the fulfilment of the divine good pleasure.

Note also what will come to pass : that
the soul, now once entered into the Divine

Will, and raised up by its aid, meets for
the time to come with no difficulty, but
the door of return is open to her at pleasure, because she has not yet solved the
secret of this business, uncovered it, and
pierced to its inmost depths; because
also she has, by her own experience,
found God, light, joy, and life; not where
she had expected, nor where most persons
are wont to seek these things, that is, in
ourselves and in our own will, and in our
own joy, light, and satisfaction. She
finds them, on the contrary, there, where
she had least supposed them, and where
they are seldom sought, in the renouncement of self, and even in the neglect of
spiritual joy, light, and pleasure. For
all these things are put in the rear, and
as it were forgotten, the thought of the
Will of God and His good pleasure, and
the immense gladness conceived therefrom, filling up all the view.

That which deters us from an absolute
renouncement of ourselves, for the sake
of the Will of God, is the opinion steal-
ing over us that by such renouncement
we shall be deprived of what we desire,
and of all that forms our delight. But
when once the soul has learned the con-

trary by experience, and has found that
by renouncement and forgetfulness of her
own will, and joy for the sake of the
Divine Will, her will and joy are not
quenched or brought to nothing, but are,
according to His promise, increased a
hundred fold; then she is no longer
sad. She now experiences no reluctance
in renouncing self, and in offering to God
her dear one, her only son Isaac, that is,
her joy and her own will, because she
foresees as a certainty that though he is
bound, and laid on the altar of the heart
in this mountain of prayer, and the sword
of justice is near falling on his head, and
he is about to be burnt by the rude fire of
renouncement, yet never will he be handed
over really to death, but he will still live,
and, according to his name, will be changed
into joy and laughter.

PRAYER OF SAINT FRANCIS,

TO BE SAID OFTEN IN THE DAY, BUT ESPECIALLY
BEFORE BEGINNING AN AFFAIR OF MOMENT,
OR ANY LENGTHY BUSINESS.

O ALMIGHTY, everlasting God, just
and merciful, for Thy own sake
give to us miserable creatures, always to
do that which we know Thee to will, and

ever to will that which is pleasing to
Thee : that being inwardly cleansed, enlightened, and inflamed by the fire of
Thy Holy Spirit, we may follow the footsteps of Thy dearly beloved Son, our
Lord Jesus Christ, and by Thine only
grace happily come to Thee, O Most
Highest, Who in perfect Trinity and in
simple Unity, livest and reignest, and art
alone most glorious, God Almighty, for
ever and ever. Amen.

ANOTHER, TO THE B. V. MARY.

O MY LADY, holy Mary, into thy
blessed trust and especial keeping,
and into the lap of thy mercy, this day,
every day, and at the hour of my depar-
ture, I commend myself, my soul, and
my body, unto thee. All my hope and
my comfort, all my straits and my mise-
ries, my life and my life's end, I entrust
to thee : that by thy most holy interces-
sion, and by thy merits, all my works
may be directed and disposed, according
to the will of thyself, and of thy Son.
Amen.

PART II.

Of the twofold state of this Exercise.

THIS twofold distinction of states is
taken for granted, from the Will of
God itself. This Will, as was stated at
the very outset, comes down to us by
steps, for we are not able to grasp it in
any other manner, nor in its entirety all
at once. And by the same steps by which
it comes down, by the same it makes us
to ascend unto God. And as it first
becomes known to us by outward things,
and through them penetrates more and
more to things within, an occasion has thus
been given for this Will to be called, first
outward, secondly *inward.* It might also
be termed, if we would use the Apostle's
language, "good." On these two degrees
we will now in their order say something.

CHAPTER I.

Of the outward Will.

THE outward Will of God is His
Divine good pleasure, known by law
and reason. It is the normal rule of all

thoughts, words, or deeds in the active life.

I say His *Divine good pleasure;* for though our good deeds are of no use to God, as the Psalmist bears witness, "*Because Thou hast no need of my goods,*" and God neither loses nor gains anything by reason of our ill or well doing, yet through His immense goodness He receives delight and pleasure whenever we do well and keep His commandments; and, on the contrary, He takes it ill and is displeased, by reason of His justice, if at any time we transgress.

I add *known,* inasmuch as He not only has a Will and good pleasure, but He also makes the same manifest to us, by discovering to us in what His Will and good pleasure consists.

I say *by law,* for it is by law that the Will of God is made evident to us. This is to be understood of law in general, not God's law only. All good laws, of whatever sort, are to be included in this term. That law is meant of which we find it written, "*If thou wilt enter into life, keep the commandments.*" Such is the law of the Church, for "*he that will not hear the Church, let him be to thee as a*

heathen man and a publican." If a man
be a Religious, the Rule, Constitutions,
and Statutes of the Order are likewise his
law, according to the words of the Psalmist : "*Vow to the Lord your God, and
render to Him.*" The commands of Pas-
tors and Superiors are also law, for it is
said : "*Obey your prelates, and be subject to them.*" The decrees of princes are
law, for our Saviour says : "*Render to
Cæsar the things that are Cæsar's.*" The
injunctions of parents are law, according
to the words, "*Honour thy father and thy
mother.*" The magistrates' orders are
law : "*For there is no power but of God ;
he that resisteth the power resisteth the
ordinance of God.*" The statutes of a
householder are law, for of them it is
decreed : "*Servants obey your masters.*"
Lastly, what is suitable to each one's
state, degree, and condition is his law,
whether he be superior or subject, master
or servant, married or unmarried, cleric,
religious, or layman.

I say that God's Will is known to us
by reason. This is not added without
cause, for in many things God's will
cannot be known by law, because there
are things not comprised in laws, which

are neither commanded nor forbidden by laws. The entering Holy Orders, marrying or remaining unmarried, going on a journey or stopping at home, sitting or standing, being silent or speaking, and a thousand other things, are of this kind, which happen every day. These things are neither commanded nor forbidden, but are left free to each one's choice: and as it is difficult in such cases to ascertain exactly what the Will of God is, recourse must be had to reason for a solution. By the term *reason* is meant discretion, godliness, and counsel. How the solution is to be obtained from reason in these doubtful matters has been shown in Part I. chapter ii.

Following the doctors, I further say that the Will of God is the *Rule of our wills, our thoughts, words, and deeds.* For as by a material rule or square a straight line is drawn, and the straightness or crookedness of anything is examined by it, so by the Will of God we can make straight the course of our whole life, the thread of our intentions, thoughts, words and deeds. By the same Will we may learn if our aim is correct, or turns aside crookedly from the straight path.

I add, lastly, *in the active life.* This term comprises the inward intention, as well as the outward action. It embraces the inward reformation, as well as the outward manner of life.

But if the question be asked, why to this Will is applied the term "outward," when it reaches to and reforms that which is within? I answer that it is because the soul seeks its light and direction from that which is without; that is, from law. On this account it concerns itself mostly with outward things; in admitting or shrinking from anything, it follows the same law. And further, although that which applies the file and the rule to the intention be within, yet not wrongfully may it be termed outward, in comparison with the two other wills, which are wholly on every side within.

CHAPTER II.

Of the inner Will of God.

SECTION I.

GOD'S inner Will is the Divine good pleasure, made clear by perfect, plain, and experimental inner knowledge, enlightening the soul in its inner or contemplative life. This it does when the soul gazes upon God and contemplates Him, and in her inmost self experiences, feels, and tastes the Divine Will, which is that pleasure and delight that God feels by the performance of such or such a thing. For when any one faithfully has directed and confirmed his intention in God's outer Will, it is impossible for him not to obtain an eminent purity of soul, which purity brings with it a certain death of the passions and affections of the soul; and that death begets a calm, the calm a deep silence, and in the silence the soul hears the voice of her Beloved knocking. By her own proper experience she perceives that *His voice is sweet, and His Face is comely."* And so she can say with the Samaritan, *"Now* we believe, not because of thy saying;"—that is, through outward instruction—"but we have ourselves heard Him, and we know that this is verily the Saviour of the world."

From this time forth the soul no longer feels and tastes her own human will and pleasure, but the Divine; being absorbed and transformed into the Will of God.

This is what S. Thomas affirms. (*De Humanitate Christi*, c. I.) As the Divine Light, growing less gradually, comes down gradually into us, so contrariwise by the same light we are brought gradually back into God by increase. That saying of the Psalmist is of the same drift : " *They shall go from virtue to virtue; the God of Gods shall be seen in Sion ;*" that is, in perfect contemplation, as the gloss has it. The Book of Proverbs also says : " *The path of the just, as a shining light, goeth forward, and increaseth, even to the perfect day ;*" which day is, according to the gloss, life everlasting.

This Will therefore shows itself to us, not in one only, but in divers manners, by degrees. We cannot all at once comprehend it, but little by little, by those degrees, which we shall sum up as five, though others might be made. These five are, manifestation, wonder, abasement, exultation, and uplifting.

SECTION II.

The first degree, which a pure outward intention gives birth to, is called *manifestation.* It comes from this cause as its

proper effect, if only the intention is
really pure, having the Divine Will as
the single aim of its work, every other
end, howsoever good, being set aside; in
short, if only the intention has the six
degrees already explained in Part I. For
when the intention has reached this
purity, it is impossible for the soul not to
have the taste of this inner Will, and to
feel its internal drawing.

For man cannot be stirred by any
motive without seeing or feeling that
motive. If then he be stirred by this
motive only he sees it or feels it; and
if he is moved by the Will of God only,
he certainly perceives this Will of God.
If he be stirred by some other motive, I
do not say a bad one, but a good one,
then he will not feel the Will of God,
though his motive may be ever else so
excellent.

Now to look close into the essence of
this purity, it is plain that it is no other
thing than a pure and free choice of
God's Will and good pleasure, made by
the soul's free will, in preference to following her own liking, passion, or self-
will, and the work she has in hand. And
this choice implies a turning away from

created things, and a simple conversion of
the soul to God.

This choice is made by a simple view
of the Divine Will : to wit, when in our
foresaid work or suffering, we, with all
calmness, gently, and without violence or
forcing, shoot the arrow of our thought or
spiritual gaze into God. This thought
and gaze are in the power of our free will,
in the higher portion, even amidst afflictions, distresses, and any works whatsoever. This ought to be a great comfort,
a strength and encouragement to those
who are dashed about, and tossed this
way and that, through the tumults of
their passions and temptations, in their
inward conflicts. And the more calm,
simple, and free from multiplicity this
view of God is made, so much the more
clearly and plainly shall we behold and
taste the Divine Will, and our mind will
sooner become single, losing every im-
press of passion, temptation, distress, and
the images of the work wrought.

This is the key to the whole contemplative life. When the soul has once
found this key, and has fully tasted of
this pleasure, then no more difficulty will
be experienced in the renouncement of

self. The acquiring the purity of intention will be no longer irksome; for it is easy to despise a good or delight that is smaller, in order to give room for one that is greater.

SECTION III.

After the manifestation of the *delight* which God gives from the performance of His Will, there follows another degree, to wit, *wonder.* This draws its birth principally from three causes. The first is God's Greatness; the second our own nothingness; the third is the amazing familiarity of God with the soul. For this inward will, into which the soul has immersed herself, and with which she has rendered herself one and the same, gives to her so vast and so true a knowledge of God, that she knows for a certainty, with clear evidence, that in all nature there is nothing else but Himself, that He is the only BEING to be found: that all the rest is nothing: for though the rest of things have a certain borrowed essence, yet she sees that they are to be esteemed as nothing when there is question of the Divine Essence, from which

their essence flows forth. For the Divine
Essence would not be Infinite if besides
it there were another, since the one would
have a bound where the other began.

Experience proves that it is the knowledge of the Divine Immensity which
begot this wonder in the soul. The wonder increases through the thought of our
our own meanness. These are so inter-
dependent, the one upon the other, that
the knowledge of the one is impossible ·
without the knowledge of the other. We
cannot ever know the infiniteness of
God's BEING, unless we know our own
nothingness ; nor can we understand our
own *nothingness* unless we have knowledge of the infiniteness of God's BEING.

But when the soul knows that immensity, she understands at the same time
her own nothingness. Then she stands
struck with amazement, and full of wonder she cries out with the prophet : " *I
am brought to nothing, and I knew not.*"

The soul tarries so long, it may be, in
this contemplation, clasped in the embrace of the Divine Being, in this Will,
that when she comes away and beholds
herself, comparing herself with this Being,
she discovers that she is but the merest

vanity, and a very nothing. This knowledge renders her free, and opens before her a clear road to God, so that she may come or go at pleasure, as the Lord affirms: "*He shall go out and come in, and find pasture.*"

These two Divine illuminations and workings are followed by a third: to wit, a singular sweet familiarity which God deigns to show to the soul. By this the soul is stricken with wonder much greater still: that the King of kings and Lord of lords should enter into familiar communication with a slave, who borrows all she has from Himself; nay, that He should converse and associate with one that is sinful and His enemy, and should woo her, and caress her, and look sweetly upon her, and lavish on her continually some fresh favour and love token: and should so behave Himself towards her as if she were so precious to Him that He could not do without her. This not only melts her into wonder, but the vehemency of her amazement ravishes her out of herself, and her mind fainting away through such love she cries out: "*Stay me with flowers:*" stay me with the flowers of the pattern of Jesus Christ. After His example I desire to renounce self-will, to become obedient unto death, to bring myself to nothing, that so I may at least pay some little tittle of my debts to this Immense Goodness. "*Comfort me with apples*" of sweet-smelling prayers; for these flowers are the pillars on which I lean, firm as adamant, lofty as heaven, deep as the abyss, lasting as eternity.

SECTION IV.

From this wonder a sudden passage is made into the next degree, that of *abasement*, so soon as the soul has beheld the Divine Immensity and Almightiness, wondering most of all at this, that she finds God is evidently everywhere. When then with most intent gaze she has contemplated Him, without her and within, above and below, on every side round about; when too she sees most plainly that God is nearer to her than she is to herself; when she knows His goodness, tastes His sweetness, perceives His kindness, obtains His intimate friendship, and experiences within her the tokens of His quick and powerful working, in sweet and secret action drawing her to Him

' with vehement force; when, in fine, together with this immensity of glory and divine goodness, she ponders over her own mean wretchedness and sin: then there come forth acts of abasement as profound as they are most secret and subtle, and she cries with the Apostle Peter: "*Depart from me, for I am a sinful man, O Lord.*" Or again, with S. Elizabeth: "*And whence is this to me?*" i.e. what goodness must I think it to be, that my Lord should come to me. Sometimes also as the Blessed Peter again she exclaims: "*Lord, dost Thou wash my feet?*" my miry earthly affections, by Thy heavenly familiar caresses. Wilt Thou, O Lord, Thou King of Glory, by the friendly sweet working of Thy Divine Will, beget in me a distaste of the bitterness of my own will? This glory of Thy Majesty is a burden to me. I cannot endure that Thy greatness should stoop so low. Such an excess of goodness is more than I can comprehend. The vehemency of Thy love I am too feeble to sustain. Depart from me, O Lord, and "*suffer me a little, that I may lament my sorrow.*" (Job x.)

But when the soul sees that to wash

her feet is really God's Will, which is her
only life and gladness, the breath of her
inmost heart, then, with an insatiable
longing to cleave only to His good pleasure, she cries : *" Lord, not my feet only ;
but also my hands and my head."* I
would have not only my feet undefiled, to
tread Thy paths ; but my understanding
enlightened to know Thy law, and my
hands harmless in the exercise of good
works.   Then, having put off the old
man, I shall not only be able to say, *" I
have washed my feet, how shall I defile
them ?"* but I shall add; *" I have put off
my garment, how shall I put it on
again ?"*   But the Spouse will answer :
*" ' He that is washed needeth not save to
wash his feet, but is wholly clean.'*   For
if thou shut out thy own affections, *' thou
art all fair, and there is no spot in thee.'*
Let Me then accomplish My Will in thee.
Suffer Me to act with thee, for *I will
espouse thee to Me in faith."*

SECTION V.

The next place after abasement is
claimed by *exultation* of mind.   For the
soul is elevated by the very same things

which bring her low. Her very nothingness, which shows before her eyes what
she is in herself, clearly reveals also how
she is all in God, and how by abandoning
the finite she may be united to the Infinite. From this she knows full well that,
as she is of herself nothing, so she cannot by herself subsist, but only by Him
Who Is, that is, God. And if it is by
Him she subsists, by Him equally is she
kept in being, and therefore He is in her
and she in Him, in whom is the true
exultation of the mind.

In like fashion also the greatness of
God, His glory and magnificence, bring
the soul down low. They also fill her
with joy, from her seeing that she is
made one and the same with them.

The familiarity of God works that lowliness which is forthwith followed by
exultation, so that she sings with Blessed
Mary, "*My spirit hath exulted in God
my Saviour; for He hath regarded the
lowliness of His handmaiden.*"

To conclude, another more essential
cause that begets this exultation is the
stupendous indissoluble union of the
human mind with God, of which it is
said that *he that cleaveth to God is one*

spirit. For when we renounce our own will we cleave and are joined to that of God, and are made one with His very Spirit and Will.

The effects of this exultation are to bring us into our interior, lead us back to it, and keep us in it. It renders sweet the renouncement of our own will, and makes us despise fleshly consolations, and forget worldly delights. We get to be above afflictions, being quiet in the midst of labours, and so carry off the victory over our hellish foes. By this exultation things which seem impossible are rendered easy; we get courage to persevere; the road to heaven is opened to us; and, in short, it gives us wings to fly to paradise. For it is of the soul that has this exultation that it is said, *"Who is she that goeth up from the desert, flowing with delights, leaning upon her Beloved,"* closely united to Him ?

SECTION VI.

The last degree, following that o exultation, is that of *uplifting;* the uplifting being in this Will, and therefore in God Himself. This uplifting is caused by all the degrees which go before it: to wit,

by Manifestation, Wonder, Abasement,
and Exultation. Manifestation first puts
before the soul (so far as she is capable of
bearing it) this Will of God, as it is in
God ; and gives it to her clearly to taste,
so that she learns by her proper experience that it is spirit and life. Now this
is a thing so high, and so surpassing all
understanding, that no ability of man or
any learning can reach so far, because it
is impossible by natural powers to get
beyond the bounding limits of nature.

It follows from hence that manifestation lifts up above nature, for it makes
plain the Will of God, the Spirit and Life.

Wonder still more lifts the soul up
above nature. For as this is nothing else
than an entire stretching of the soul, and
all her powers, into what is beyond and
above the sphere of their activity, it follows that this wonder lifts up the soul
affected by it. For this kind of stretching of herself, and complete application of
her faculties to the Will of God, implies,
on the one hand, a turning away from
outer things by a complete gathering
together of the senses and their powers ;
and on the other a perfect clinging and
cleaving of the soul to this Will, so as to

4

grasp it altogether. Now, from this turning away, and turning to, or adhesion, is
born this Uplifting.

Again, with regard to Abasement, this
too lifts up the soul, not only to grace,
virtue, and the favour of God, but also to
the actual contemplation and experimental knowledge of Him. For man by such
abasement having brought himself and all
other things to nothing, thence sees God
in all things, so that he sees only God.
In this consists the true Uplifting.

The same must be said of Exultation,
for it is nothing else but an immense joy
and spiritual gladness, whose lavish
plenty beyond measure fills the soul, in-
toxicating her so with its delicious sweetness as to sweep out of her memory the
entire world. Then, forgetful of herself
and of all created things, she is wholly
steeped in God, the well-spring of joys.
He so occupies all her faculties, and
sweetly wounds her heart, He claims such
a full possession of her, that stripped and
despoiled of all right and dominion over
herself, she follows His footsteps, gives
ear to His words, holds fast to His teaching, and abandons herself to Him altogether. She clings wholly to His good

pleasure, follows Him as a shadow the body, sticks to Him as an accident to its substance, as the circumference to its centre, a limb to the body, a branch to the vine, a part to the whole. Thus she is made one and the same spirit with Him, for " *he who is joined to the Lord is one Spirit.*"

From what has been said it is now plain that this Inner Will does not arrive in the soul in its fulness all at once, but comes by degrees, little and little. Without its presence the soul is as the world, veiled on all sides with the thick darkness of night. This Will is like the sun of day. When it arises darkness disappears, and the world grows brighter and brighter. For this Will brings to the soul such floods of glistening light, that emerging from the abyss of darkness, she is brought to the perfect contempla-tion of God, that true Sun, with which the woman in the Apocalypse was clothed. Then the Angels, beholding the soul clad with light as with a garment, cry again and again in admiration: " *Who is she that cometh forth as the morning rising, fair as the moon, bright as the sun, ter-rible as an army set in array ?*"

CONCLUSION.

INASMUCH as the Passion of our Lord
Jesus Christ is so necessary as to
form an essential part of this Rule, that
must not be passed over in silence which
is said in Holy Scripture: "Look, and
make it according to the pattern that was
shown to thee in the mount." Doctors say
that this means that we should always
have the Passion before our eyes. How
much God would have this contemplation
of Him commended to us is to be seen
from the very words. From the first
word, "Look," He enjoins a fixed searching gaze and consideration. He does this
because in the Passion many things be
hid within, not being seen outside; and
it is only by a good, fixed, long, and
watchful scrutiny that they are discovered.
. The words likewise "make it according
to the pattern," make clear our necessity
to look to the Passion, which is our pattern and prototype, to behold as a
painter each trait of the pencil of virtue,
good works, or endurance; and never to
attempt anything without first paying

attention to this model, for fear of making ourselves to differ from this pattern.

There seems therefore a lack of humility in that soul, which, despising the Passion of the Lord, would be carried to His Godhead only. Besides, it is no small disadvantage, for in time of tribulation, adversity, and affliction, she has no prop to support her; so that hanging in the air, as it were, she is carried about everywhere by the violence of the tempest.

However, it must be observed that the Manhood is not to be contemplated by itself: but with it the Godhead. In this point many err. For either they contemplate only the Manhood, or they think they should by turns contemplate the Manhood and the Godhead by different looks. From this it happens therefore that some get despondent, fancying almost that there is no other mystery than that while contemplating Christ's Manhood they should fix before their eyes some one tortured on the Cross. They think that to behold His Godhead they must dismiss what they were looking on, because they imagine it impossible to look on both the Godhead and the Manhood at the same time. It is true that to do so requires a subtle vision; for to behold God and Man with the same simple view is much the same as the knowledge that God and Man form but one same Person. All the difficulty of this contemplation proceeds from the seeming contradiction to the reason of man, of being able to behold, at one single view, God and Man, body and spirit. For to behold the Manhood, which is bodily, there is need of images: but to contemplate the Godhead images must be stripped off, and the soul placed in abstraction. It seems therefore that to be able to see both at once would require that the soul should, at the same time, use images and be bare of images. This, then, with many is the "rock of stumbling."

In order, then, to loose this knot, we ought to transcend reason entirely, and rise to faith. Faith, whilst it sees our Lord to be Man, at the same time acknowledges Him to be God, who has neither form nor image. And though the imagination suggest the form of man, faith, passing all sense, considers no form, for it fixes its eyes on God. Thus though the representation of the crucifix offers itself to us, yet the immensity of faith swallows it up, and brings it to nought.

It being laid down that in the contemplation of the Passion the soul beholds in one Person God and Man too, there still rests the no small doubt whether it be best to look on the Crucified under the form in which He once suffered at Jerusalem, or under the form of actual pains, bitternesses, and afflictions, which each one experiences in himself.

Now, though both modes are highly to be approved, the latter seems preferable to the former: that is, to those who are capable of it, but not to all men. For that real suffering which we experience in ourselves is to us a far livelier picture of the Passion of Jesus Christ than that which is only the work of the imagination. It is on this account that S. Bonaventure says (*Serm. Div. Amor.* p. 9, c. 2): By sufferings man learns to compassionate the suffering. Besides, if when combatting with distresses we run to the Passion of Christ as outside of us, we shall evidently seem to turn our backs on our pains, and to shun, as far as we may, our torments, since we turn to Him very often, drawn by our own comfort rather

than by true love of Him. But when in
our pains we perceive Him within us,
then we easily embrace our bitterness as
His, and seek eagerly the sharp point of
affliction, as that which nails and fastens
us to Him on the Cross.

But it must be specially noted, that
when we contemplate Christ's Passion
within ourselves, we must contemplate
only the pains and afflictions. For to
seek, or even to admit, sensible consola-
tion, would be to open wide the door to
illusions. The pains and troubles therefore are not to be taken as one's own, but
as those of Jesus Christ. He is to be
considered and contemplated as crucified
in us. All our pains, afflictions, and
every ill, whether of body or soul, are to
be cast together into the burning fiery
furnace of the torments of Jesus. There
they are to be wholly consumed and
united to His pains; so that we might
say with the Apostle, "with Christ I am
nailed to the cross;" obeying the injunc-
tion, "let this mind be in you, which was
also in Christ Jesus."

In all these things is this practice the
more perfect. Still, since different persons have differing devotions, it is not

advisable that all souls should be bound
to this method, especially those who have
not yet penetrated far into the Godhead,
though in other respects they have made
good spiritual progress, for such are unable to perceive how God is in their
afflictions.

When the soul has become thus well
stablished in the practice of the Passion, there then arises another doubt,
namely, whether she ought to abandon
its contemplation, so as to rise to that of
the Godhead only.*

To this it must be answered, that she
ought not to abandon the Passion in
order to contemplate the Godhead, but
should at one and the same time contemplate both.

2. She ought not to abandon the Pas-

---

* It is a disputed point among contemplative
writers, whether, when the soul is drawn to the contemplation of the Godhead, the images of the Passion
should be relinquished. S. Teresa and some moderns,
with our author, say the images of the Passion
should always be retained. S. Augustine, S. Gregory,
S. Bernard, and all the Benedictine school, are of the
opposite opinion. Blosius and Father Baker in this
matter follow the ancient tradition. The Capuchin
Father Balduke, in his "Kingdom of God in the
Soul," chapter xxv., teaches not to think of the
Passion, except by a formless image. This is a sort
of compromise between the two schools of teaching.

sion, even though the way upwards is
quite open, and though the soul seem
drawn aloft.

3. The contemplation of the Passion is
of all the most perfect and sublime. For
how can any one be supposed to love
Jesus Christ if he turn his back to Him,
as He hangs on the cross, that removed
from the sight of Him he may be free for
the lofty contemplation of the Godhead ?
Not only ought we not to seek by our
own industry to withdraw from the Passion in order to contemplate the Godhead ; but, further, we should not allow
ourselves to be drawn away to it, though
some disposition for it, and an opening to
it, seems to offer.

For if for every seeming upward drawing we should be obliged to leave the
Passion, we should never be able to
sound its depths, or penetrate into its
mystery. In order thoroughly to contemplate the Passion, we must have in view
both the loftiness of the Godhead and the
lowliness of the Manhood. Both must
be before us, not the Godhead only.
When a man mounts up a tree, if he
looks at its top only, and never casts his
eyes to its roots, he cannot judge of its

height, so he who ascends into the lofty
tree of the mystery of the Incarnation
cannot behold its height if he looks only
at the Godhead, without attending to the
sorrowful and despised Human Nature.

Now, as the Godhead and Manhood are
knit together in one Person, so are they
to be contemplated, not separately, but
by one same simple view. It is very
clear that this contemplation is the most
perfect; for in it the Godhead gives illu-
mination in contemplation, and the Manhood instructs in active working by its
example. As then to contemplate, and to
deliver what we have contemplated to
others—that is the contemplative and active life joined—is a more perfect thing
than the contemplative life by itself; so
the contemplation of the Godhead and
Manhood at once, as found in the Passion, contained more perfection than the
abstracted contemplation of the Godhead
only.

In order then to the consideration of
the Passion, after the manner of this
exercise, the Godhead and Manhood must
be ever conjointly beheld. The object
before the eyes must be God Crucified.
For as in the first stage we work and

suffer that the Will of God may be done; so in this second we act and suffer that God may be in us; that is, that He may live and reign. In the first, whilst we work the Will of God is almost connected with suffering, because things repugnant to nature have to be accepted, and things pleasing to be rejected; so in the second, God and the Cross are almost always together; because the same rule of accepting and rejecting has to be followed. Again, as in the first the Divine Will and suffering, or the Cross and affliction, are one and the same thing; so in the second, Godhead and His Cross are also one. And since, in the first, the Will of God, or affliction and the cross, without any multiplicity, are to be contemplated; so in the second, God and His Cross are to be contemplated in the one same and simple view.

May God give peace in our days.

www.ingramcontent.com/pod-product-compliance
Lightning Source LLC
Chambersburg PA
CBHW020238090426
42735CB00010B/1743